THE LIFE OF FLORENCE NIGHTINGALE

Liz Gogerly

WAYLAND

Text copyright © Liz Gogerly

Project manager: Louisa Sladen
Designer: Peta Morey

First published in 2003 by Hodder Wayland,
an imprint of Hodder Children's Books

This paperback edition published in 2006

Reprinted in 2007, 2008, 2010 and 2011 by Wayland

British Library Cataloguing in Publication Data
Gogerly, Liz
The life of Florence Nightingale. - (Beginning history)
1. Nightingale, Florence, 1820-1910 - Juvenile literature
2. Nurses - Great Britain - Biography - Juvenile literature
3. Crimean War, 1853-1856 - Medical care - Great Britain - Juvenile literature
I. Title
610.7'3'092

ISBN: 978 0 7502 4428 2

Printed and bound in China

Hachette Children's Books
338 Euston Road, London NW1 3BH

Picture Acknowledgements
The publishers would like to thank the following for allowing their pictures to be
reproduced in this publication: The Yale Centre for British Art/Bridgeman Art Library
p7; Christie's Images Ltd [1993] p13; Mary Evans Picture Library cover, title page,
p4, p16; The Florence Nightingale Museum Trust p3, p6, p8, p10, p14, p15 (top),
p15 (bottom), p19 (top), p19 (bottom), p20, p23; Wayland Picture Library p11, p21
(bottom); Peter Newark's Military Pictures p17; Popperfoto p5; Science
Museum/Science & Society Picture Library p18; Topham p9, p21 (top).

Cover: In Scutari, Florence Nightingale attends a patient.
Painting dated 1854-5, artist unknown.

While every effort has been made to secure permission, in some cases it has
proved impossible to trace copyright holders.

Wayland is an imprint of Hachette Children's Book,
an Hachette UK Company.

www.hachette.co.uk

Contents

Young Florence

Florence Nightingale was born on 12 May 1820. Her parents were on holiday in Italy at the time. They named her after the beautiful city of Florence where she was born. Florence had a happy childhood. Her family were wealthy and she had a good education. She was clever and attractive, but she was also caring.

In **Victorian** England girls from rich families were expected to marry and have children. Nobody thought they should have a **career**. Florence often dreamed about her future. Surely there was more to life than being somebody's wife? She longed to do a job that would help other people.

▲ **Lea Hurst in Derbyshire was Florence's favourite home. Her family had houses in Hampshire and London too.**

Florence with her pet ▶ owl, Athena. This sketch is a copy of a drawing by Florence's sister, Parthenope.

Hospitals and Germs

When Florence was a young woman many people died from diseases like **cholera**, **typhus** and **tuberculosis**. There were no **medicines** to cure these illnesses. People did not know that disease is caused by **germs**. They didn't realize that germs grow best in dirty **conditions**.

Poor people often lived in dirty, overcrowded places where diseases were spread easily.
▼

▲ This cartoon is of a patient and his drunken nurse. It shows how many people thought of nurses in Victorian times.

Victorian hospitals were full of germs. Doctors used dirty **equipment** and did not wash their hands. Nobody wore a uniform and the nurses were not **trained** to look after the patients. Florence said that nursing was done by those 'who were too old, too weak, too drunken, too dirty…or too bad to do anything else.'

A Job for a Lady?

At nineteen Florence fell in love, but she did not want to get married. Her parents sent her off to Europe for a holiday. They hoped she would change her mind.

When she visited a hospital in Germany, Florence made up her mind! She decided she would become a nurse. In those days people thought nursing was not a good job for a lady. Florence had terrible arguments with her parents about it. Finally, they agreed to let Florence begin **training** as a nurse. She worked very hard, but Florence was happy. At last, she was helping other people.

Florence with her sister, ▶ Parthenope. Parthenope was very angry with her sister when Florence said she wanted to become a nurse.

A collection of things that belonged to Florence when she was a child. Can you see the snake's skin and shells that she found on holiday?
▼

9

The War in the Crimea

In 1853, Florence became the **manager** of a hospital in London. She was good at **organizing** people. She made lots of useful changes to the hospital. Next, she began looking at ways of improving nursing.

French soldiers lead an attack on the Russians during the Crimean War.

Then, in 1854, the **Crimean War** began. England, France and Turkey were fighting against Russia. Thousands of wounded British soldiers were dying in the hospitals in the **Crimea**. There were not enough doctors, and there were no nurses to look after the soldiers. The **government** asked Florence to take a group of nurses out to the Crimea to help.

▲ The picture above shows a Russian hospital in the Crimea. But conditions in hospital would have been just as bad for British soldiers.

The Nightmare at Scutari

Florence and her nurses arrived at the hospital at Scutari in November 1854. They were shocked by what they saw. The hospital was filthy and filled with rats. There were not enough beds for the soldiers, who were very ill. There was not even any proper food for the poor men.

Florence was desperate to help the soldiers. But at first, the doctors did not want her or her group of nurses to go near them. So the women cleaned the hospital instead. Then they **organized** a kitchen and made tasty soups for the sick soldiers.

Florence welcomes injured soldiers into Scutari Hospital. One of the other nurses offers a wounded soldier some water. ▶

The Lady with the Lamp

Very soon, the doctors asked Florence and her nurses to help look after the men. Each evening, Florence made her **rounds** of the hospital with a lamp in her hand. She walked along miles of dark corridors so that she could talk to all the sick soldiers. Florence's care for them made the soldiers feel much better.

Florence and her nurses helped to clean Scutari Hospital. It became a much more comfortable place for its patients.

Back in England people heard about Florence's good work. A poem was written about her called 'The Lady with the Lamp'. Meanwhile, Florence was working so hard that she became ill. Her family begged her to come home but Florence kept working until 1856 when the war was over.

▲ Florence had become so famous that special china figures of her were made. People bought them and put them in their homes.

◄ This Victorian medicine chest belonged to Florence. Can you see the scales she used to measure the medicine?

Making Hospitals Better

Florence nearly died while she was out in the **Crimea**. But when she came home she kept on working. Now she wanted to make the **conditions** in army hospitals better. She wrote thousands of letters to **government ministers**, doctors, and heads of hospitals and colleges.

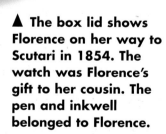

▲ The box lid shows Florence on her way to Scutari in 1854. The watch was Florence's gift to her cousin. The pen and inkwell belonged to Florence.

◄ When Florence came home she looked very thin. Her hair was short, because it had been cut when she was ill.

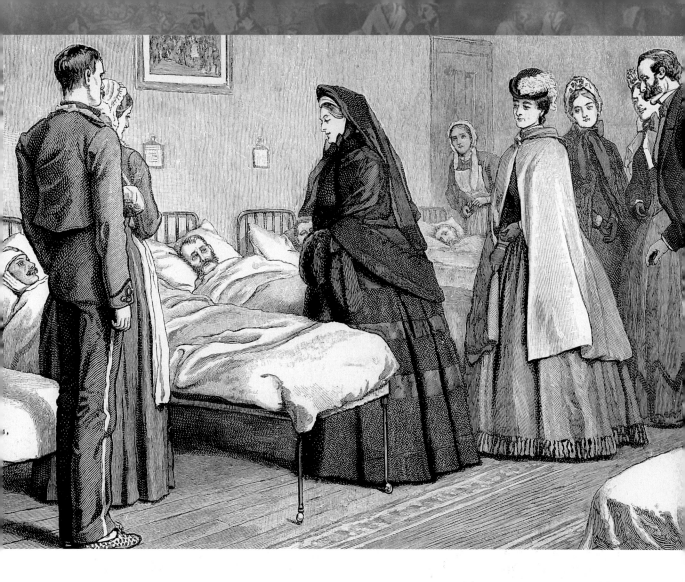

Florence's hard work paid off. In 1860, a new Army Medical School was opened and the conditions in soldiers' **barracks** and hospitals everywhere **improved**. Florence spent most of the rest of her life in bed or lying on a sofa. Even so, she never stopped thinking and writing about how hospitals should be run.

▲ In this picture, Queen Victoria is visiting sick soldiers in hospital in 1870. Thanks to Florence, hospitals were slowly beginning to improve.

The Nightingale Nurses

Florence wrote a book about her new ideas. She said that cleanliness was very important in hospitals. She suggested that patients' beds be placed near windows. She believed that patients should be treated well. Allowing them to have visitors would cheer them up. She also said that visitors should take flowers to the patients.

By the end of Queen Victoria's reign, most doctors and nurses wore uniforms, and surgical equipment was properly cleaned.

▼

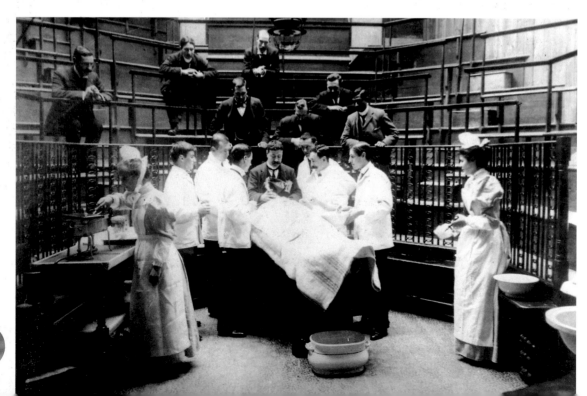

▲ Florence in 1886 with a group of nurses doing their training. She wrote letters to many of the nurses giving them advice.

Florence suggested that the nurse's uniform ▶ should include a white cap and an apron.

In 1860, Florence opened the Nightingale Training School for Nurses in London. For the first time, nurses were given proper **training** in caring for the sick. The school became very successful. The same kind of training schools were set up throughout the world.

Why We Remember Florence Nightingale

Florence lived until she was ninety years old. When she died in August 1910, people thought she should be buried in **Westminster Abbey** in London, because she had done so much for sick people. But Florence had chosen to be buried next to her parents in the village churchyard.

In 1861, Florence fell ill and nearly died. For the rest of her life she was never very strong: but she did live to be a very old lady. ▶

Florence spent only two years of her life as a nurse in the **Crimea**, but that is the part of her life that people remember best. She is important because she helped to plan modern hospitals. Most of all, it is thanks to Florence Nightingale that nurses are now properly **trained** to care for us all.

▲ Modern nurses are trained to care for their patients. Many men as well as women now train to become nurses.

◀ A statue of Florence carrying a lamp stands in front of St Thomas's Hospital in London.

Glossary

Barracks These are the buildings used by soldiers for living and sleeping in.

Career When people choose to do the same kind of job all their working life, then they have a career. Florence Nightingale had a career in nursing.

Cholera A dangerous disease that is passed between people. Victims get sickness and diarrhoea.

Conditions The state of a place. The conditions at a hospital would be described as good if it was clean and well-heated.

Crimea A region of land in the Ukraine, between the Black Sea and the Sea of Azov. It was part of Russia until 1991.

Crimean War The war was fought in the Crimea. It was a series of battles between Russia on one side and England, France, Turkey and Sardinia on the other. It lasted from 1853 to 1856.

Equipment The different tools that doctors use to treat their patients, such as thermometers.

Germs Tiny living things that can cause illness. Germs are passed from one person to another by coughing or by breathing in the same air. Germs cause all kinds of different illnesses.

Government A group of people who decide how a country is run.

Government ministers These people make the country's laws. These laws are rules which everyone has to obey.

Improving, Improved Making things better.

Manager The person who is in charge of a business, or a place where lots of people work, such as a hospital.

Medicines Liquid or tablets that are given to sick people to make them better.

Organizing, Organized Planning and deciding how something should be done.

Rounds The visits to their patients that doctors and nurses make.

Training, Trained Being given lessons at a school or college on how to do a job properly.

Tuberculosis A serious disease that is passed between people. Victims' lungs are usually affected.

Typhus A disease that is caused by germs in food and water. Victims get headaches and fever.

Victorian Queen Victoria ruled England from 1837 to 1901. Anything that was made during her reign is called Victorian. Hospitals built during that time are called Victorian hospitals.

Westminster Abbey A church in London where all English kings and queens are crowned. Many important people are buried there.

Further Information

Books to Read

A Picture Book of Florence Nightingale by David A. Adler, John Wallner and Alexander Wallner
(Holiday House, 1997)

Florence Nightingale (in the Life Stories series) by Nina Morgan
(Hodder Wayland, 1995)

Florence Nightingale by Jane Shuter
(Heinemann, 2001)

Famous Lives: Florence Nightingale by Kay Barnham (Hodder Wayland, 2003)

Places to Visit

**The Florence Nightingale Museum
2 Lambeth Palace Road,
London, SE1 7EW
(Telephone: 020 7620 0374)**
– school groups are welcomed at this museum which has many objects that belonged to Florence Nightingale. Special activities for school children help to make this a lively learning experience.

**Florence Nightingale's Grave
St Margaret's Churchyard,
East Wellow, Romsey,
Hampshire, SO51 6BH**
– you can see the place where Florence is buried next to her family and her gravestone with its simple inscription: 'F.N. Born 1820. Died 1910'.

Index